Published by
Robert Boyd Publications
260 Colwell Drive, Witney
Oxfordshire OX28 5LW

First published 2007

Copyright © Derek Honey and
Robert Boyd Publications

ISBN: 978 1 899536 80 1

All drawings and most photographs
are by the author. Those that are not
are acknowledged.

L

and

BREWERIES
Past and Present

DEREK HONEY

R. Gillibrand

Front cover: Wychwood Brewery, *back cover:* Making Beer in Witney, *above:* Market Square.

Above: Church Green dominated by St Mary's Church.
Right: The Buttercross, Witney's famous landmark.

Contents

Preface

Currently Witney has 26 public houses, that is places open to the public between certain hours for the sale and consumption of alcohol, a ratio of one pub to every thousand persons, which is about the national average. It also has numerous licensed clubs, restaurants, public halls, off licences and supermarkets all of which sell alcohol.

However, at the turn of the 20th century Witney had 35 pubs with a population of only 3,600 people, a ratio of one to 100. In 1906, due to pressure from the Temperance Societies, two were closed, the Jolly Tucker in West End and the Malt Shovel in Corn Street.

Others have closed for various reasons. Since 1830 several licensing acts were imposed on tenants and breweries backed by the temperance societies, whose members had infiltrated the magistrates' benches. Later the first of the Defence of the Realm Acts (DORA) on the outbreak of World War I gave magistrates the power to restrict opening hours and even to suppress some pubs. The result was that many publicans could not make a living. The brewers also suffered when the Government restricted brewing to save on fuel and imported barley. The 1921 Licensing Act further restricted opening hours. All pubs had to close by 2 p.m. in the afternoon, while evening hours were only permitted between 6 p.m. to 9 p.m. or 7 p.m. to 10 p.m. The loss of sales forced many breweries to close some of their pubs. This restriction on afternoon opening was not fully lifted until 1988.

During World War I young men were also leaving to join the armed services and over three-quarters of a million died - the lost generation. Also between 1918 to 1920 Britain fell victim to 'Spanish Flu' in which 150,000 people died, mainly young persons. The combination of both these events meant that many pubs lost their most loyal customers with a surplus of women over men, who, in those days were not encouraged to go into pubs. After the war in 1920 the economy slumped and more than a million people lost their jobs. Men who survived the war were coming out of the army to go straight into being unemployed. With no spare money to spend in the pubs, yet more pubs and breweries were closed.

More recently many small breweries have been taken over by bigger concerns and then asset-stripped of their property portfolios turning breweries and pubs into housing. It has been estimated that throughout the country 20 pubs close each week while the sensible drink-driving laws have resulted in the loss of many country pubs. The Government have now banned smoking in all pubs and brewers and publicans are forecasting that yet more will close as a result

All the pubs listed in this book are in alphabetical order with the existing and past pubs having their separate chapters. I have also included for the first time a chapter on Witney's breweries .

Derek Honey
Witney, 2007

Acknowledgements

When compiling a book of such varied information many people, books and organisations have to be consulted. All of which have to be checked for accuracy as far as possible. When recalling the names and locations of pubs from long ago the present generation have to rely on the information given to them by their grandparents and in some cases, great-grandparents. When written details no longer exist human memory has to be relied on without verification.

Various Witney people and organisations have helped me in my researches in the past and more recently and I list them below. If I have missed any then it is not intentional although every effort has been made to trace the original source.

Rachel Gillibrand who was a great help with some of the photographs

Various papers published by *The Witney Historical and Archaeological Society.*

Witney Library

Victoria County History

Records of the *Witney Gazette* and the *Oxford Mail*

Witney Ghosts by Joe Robinson

Michael French

Wychwood Brewery for supplying the front and back cover photographs.

I am also grateful to Robert boyd my publisher for once more having the faith to publish yet another of my books. Also to Marjorie Affleck who has patiently read the manuscript from first draft to last, correcting the numerous errors on my part.

CHAPTER ONE

The origins of pub names and signs

Giving British pubs a name can, like many things, be traced back to the Roman occupation of our island. The sign for a Roman tavern was a bunch of ivy and vine leaves always associated with Bacchus the God of Wine. The chequers board was also a Roman sign for a place where games of chance were played. As the owner frequently lent money later moneylenders and banks adopted this sign. Our word cheque comes from that origin. As the inns and taverns dealt in cash some publicans sometimes lent out money or gave credit (the slate), they too used the chequers board as a sign and it is perhaps our oldest pub sign.

This worked well until travel became more wide-spread, hamlets developing into villages, villages into towns and cities so some form of individual identification became necessary. As few of the population could read or write the simplest way was to display a pictorial sign on the premises. This not only applied to taverns but to other trades as well. The shoe indicated a cobbler, a blacksmith a horseshoe, bakers displayed a loaf often made out of wood or iron, while barbers, who were also primitive surgeons, placed a striped red and white pole outside their shops. This represented a blood-red limb swathed in white bandages. At least one barber in Witney retains the sign.

The idea of signs originally came from the battlefield. At the height of any hand-to-hand fighting it was often difficult to distinguish friend from foe. So the leaders of these men adopted a crest on their banners or surcoats that covered their armour and these designs were the origins of coats of arms.

By the 14th century tradesmen and innkeepers found that just to show the sign of their trade was not enough, particularly in areas where the same trades congregated in specialised streets. So trade boards became more elaborate and bigger.

In 1393, Richard II made it compulsory for all innkeepers to display a sign but not tradesmen. Competition from neighbouring taverns forced signs to become even more elaborate often stretching across the street. They became dangerous for pedestrians and particularly to horseback riders.

When Charles II retook the throne he decreed that no sign should hang across the road but this did not stop the practice. So, in 1797 George III made it illegal to have a sign that projected into the road or were considered dangerous. Many tradesmen removed their signs but as it was still illegal for innkeepers not to display a sign the taverns and pubs kept theirs.

With restrictions on signs it became necessary to find something to replace them. In 1787 Paris had developed a system of numbering houses and naming streets. In Britain it was not until 1805, when many more people could read, the law enforced the numbering of houses. Even so, house numbering was not adopted in Witney until 1906. Technically it is still an offence not to display a number on your house.

Street naming and numbering greatly improved finding where you wanted to go, especially for the post. In the past post could be collected or delivered to an inn or posting house. This often required elaborate addresses, such as: "To the gentleman, Master Joseph Blogings, who liveth near the Bull over the road from the Globe and the same street as the Royal Oak, in the town of Stratford in Warwickshire. To be collected by the same gentleman at the Bull" Far better to post the letter to J. Blogings Esq., 54, The Avenue, Stratford, Warwickshire.

The naming of pubs and taverns came in many different forms. Religious signs, through their former church connections were always popular, with names such as the Cross Keys, the sign of St. Peter and an abbot and the New Inn after the inn in which Christ was born.

The most common name for a pub in Britain is the Red Lion - most towns and cities have one. This name is heraldic from the crest of John Gaunt. The Bear from the Earls of Warwick and of course names associated with royalty, particularly if the inn was on Crown property. Hence the many Crown inns. Beasts and birds depicted on crests also became popular as did the names of various Kings and Queens. Names such as the King's Head or Arms were often changed when a king died to be replaced with a Queen's Head or Arms. Charles II has more pub names associated with him than any other monarch usually named the Royal Oak. When he fled from the Battle of Worcester in 1651 he eluded capture by hiding in an oak tree at Boscobel.

Other signs recall the days of the stagecoach which always had names written on their doors. Good examples of that were the Flying Machine and the Coach and Horses. With the advent of the railways many inns, particularly near railway stations, were named after a particular locomotive or the company who operated the line. The Great Western Hotel, the Royal Scot or simply the Railway Inn are just a few names. At one time Witney had a pub called the Rocket even though it was nowhere near the rail station.

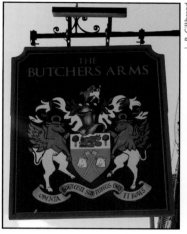

R. Gillibrand

More often than not many landlords had a second trade to boost their income so naturally they named their pubs after their trades. The Carpenters Arms, the Baker's Arms, the Butcher's Arms, the Potter's Arms and the Plumber's Arms classic examples. Out in the rural countryside pubs were named with agricultural connections. Such as the Plough, the Hand and Shears, the Fleece, the Three Horseshoes, the Wheatsheaf or the Woolpack. Locally at Curbridge the Lord Kitchener was until 1905 called the Herd of Swine.

Many publicans named their pubs after famous people or war heroes, The Nelson and Wellington being the most popular. The Duke of York, the second son of George III who as head of the British Army, has several pubs named after him. The many George inns represent the various Hanoverian kings with the Victoria pubs after that queen, often linking up with her husband, Prince Consort Albert to make the Victoria and Albert. However it is an unwritten rule that no pubs are named after a current monarch during their lifetime. Hence there are no pubs called Queen Elizabeth II although there is nothing to stop pubs being called the Prince of Wales. In practice those that do are called after a previous Prince of Wales.

Publicans needed little excuse to change the name of their pub to suit their changing clientele, a practice that has continued to the present day. Often to try and encourage the younger trade, the Slug and Lettuce perhaps being the worst example.

Some typical Witney Pub signs

' R. Gillibrand

' R. Gillibrand

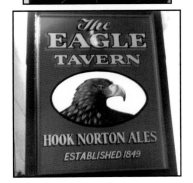

' R. Gillibrand

LIST OF WITNEY INNS AND PUBS PAST AND PRESENT

*+ Denotes closed   * Change of name   P page number in book*

Anchor + P37	Bridge Street
Angel P15	42, Market Square
Axe + P37	Newland
Bear + * P45	32, Market Square
(Lamb and Flag)	
Bell + P37	57, Corn Street
Black's Head + * P38	Bridge Street (Black Moor)
Black Horse + P38	72, West End
Black Moor + * P38	26, Bridge Street
Black Prince + * P39	63, High Street (Prince of Wales)
Black Swan + (?) * P39	Ducklington Lane or Corn Street
(New Inn ?)	
Blue Boar * P39	28, Market Square
(Marlborough Hotel)	
Border of Love + P39	Marlborough Lane
Boar's Head + *P39	46, Market Square (Bull)
Britannia + P40	53, High Street
Bull + P40	46, Market Square
Butcher's Arms P17	104, Corn Street
Carpenter's Arms + P40	Corn Street
Carpenter's Arms P18	Newland
Central Hotel + * P40	High Street (Temperance Hotel)
Chequers P18	47, Corn Street
Clothmaker's Arms + P41	Not known (Mill Street?)
Coach and Horses + P41	Marlborough Lane
Court Inn * P19	41, Bridge Street
(Old Court Hotel)	
Cross Keys P20	1, Market Square
Crown + P41	Newland
Crown Hotel + P41	27, Market Square
Czar of Russia *P42	31, West End (House of Windsor)
Dolphin + P42	Not known (Bridge Street?)
Duke's Head * P24	11, Church Green (Fleece)
Eagle Tavern P21	22, Corn Street

11

Eagle Vaults P22	20, Market Square
Elm Tree P23	21, West End
Fat Lil's P24	64a Corn Street
Fleece P24	11, Church Green
George + * P43	63, High Street (Prince of Wales)
George + P43	Newland
George and Dragon + P43	Church Green
Gibbet's Head + * P43	Market Square (Lamb & Flag)
Greyhound *P15	42, Market Square (Angel)
Golden Balls + P43	Not known
Griffin P25	Newland
Hare and Hounds + P43	Newland
Harriers + P43	15, West End
Hen and Chickens + P43	Hen and Chickens Lane, Corn Street
Hollybush P26	35, Corn Street
House of Windsor P26	West End
Izi P27	Market Square
Jolly Tucker + P43	10, West End
Jolly Waggoners + P44	High Street
King of Prussia * P44	31, West End (House of Windsor)
King's Arms + P44	106, High Street
King's Head + P45	74, High Street
Lamb + * P45	32, Market Square (Lamb & Flag)
Lamb and Flag + P45	32, Market Square
Malt Shovel + P47	17, Corn Street
Marlborough Hotel P27	Market Square
Marlborough Head * P24	Church Green (Fleece)
Mitre * P47	1, Market Square (Cross Keys)
Moor's Head + * P47	26, Bridge Street (Black Moor)
Nag's Head + P47	100, Corn Street
Nelson + P47	West End
New Inn P28	111, Corn Street
Nortons P29	Langdale Court

Old Town Arms + * P48	32, Market Square (Lamb and Flag)
Old Court Hotel * P19	Bridge Street (Court Inn)
Plasterer's Arms + P48	Newland
Plough P30	98, High Street
Prince Albert * + P38	Bridge Street (Black Moor)
Prince of Wales + P48	63, High Street
Queen's Head + P48	10, High Street
Red Lion Hotel P31	1, Corn Street
Robin Hood P31	Hailey Road
Rocket Tavern + P49	Corn Street (Star?)
Roebuck + P49	Corn Street or West End
Rosedean Hotel + P49	Church Green
Rowing Machine P32	Windrush Valley Estate
Royal Oak P32	7, High Street
Salutation * P49	1, Market Square (Cross Keys)
Saracen's Head + * P49	26, Bridge Street (Black Moor)
Staple Hall + P49	32, Bridge Street
Star + P50	152, Corn Street
Star + P50	Newland
Sundial + P50	49, Market Square
Swan + P51	Newland
Talbot + P51	Not known
Tallow Chandler's Arms + P51	Not known (Corn Street ?)
Temperance Hotel + P51	High Street
Three Horseshoes P33	78, Corn Street
Three Pigeons P34	31, Woodgreen
Union + P52	West End
Waggon and Horses + P52	Corn Street (Star ?)
Weaver's Arms + P52	West End
Wheatsheaf + P52	Not known
White Hart + P52	Bridge Street
White Lion + P53	Bridge Street
Windrush Inn P35	Burford Road

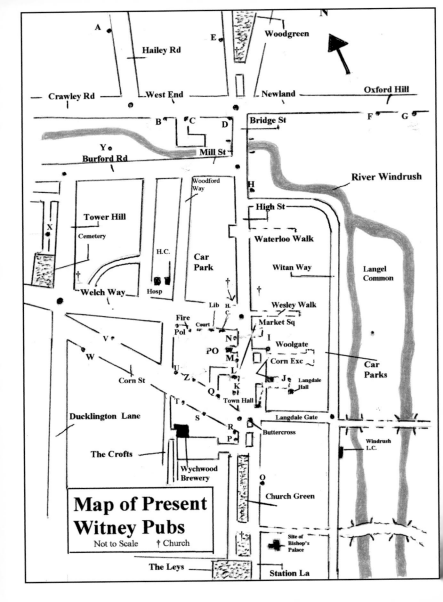

Map of Present Witney Pubs

Not to Scale   † Church

CHAPTER TWO

Present Pubs and Inns

THE ANGEL (Map P) Market Square.

Originally a baker's shop in the 17th century it became a beerhouse known as The Greyhound but when it was sold to Joseph Masters in 1809 he changed the name to The Angel. The reason for its change in name is unknown but with the town's close association with the Church and St Mary's Church at the end of Church Green it probably seemed obvious to him.

Yet perhaps he renamed it after an alleged statue of an angel that once stood on the site of the Buttercross. The Angel is a common pub name where a church is in the proximity. Indeed it was the monks of the church who first brewed ale for foot-weary pilgrims travelling to the various saints' shrines. When the Abbot's Hall became too crowded with these pilgrims the monks soon established halls outside the monastery to cater for the common pilgrim, the first recognisable pubs. So it is little wonder that so many pubs have religious names, like Friar's Head, Mitre, The Ark etc.

The church in the middle ages had many opportunities to provide refreshment for the local serfs and controlled the industry to a certain extent. During that time there were 95 saints' days and holidays as well as Idle Wakes, Church Ales, Whitsun Ales, Clerks' Ales, Helpe Ales and Bride Ales, all the ale provided - and sold - by the church. Their brewhouses became known as *Church House Inn* and even today wherever there is an ancient inn close to a church it is a sure bet that it was once owned by the church. Unfortunately that is not the case with Witney's Angel.

An interesting story connected to The Angel is of a certain local man called Albert who was keen on the ladies, married or not. He was having an affair with the wife of a local businessman and lay preacher who lived in Corn Street. Unfortunately the husband came home early one day to find his wife in bed with the man. He in turn jumped out of the window but landed in a load of horse manure. Running down Corn Street he entered the Angel and sat down at his usual stool at the bar. It was the smell that gave him away for the husband was able to trace him to the pub and immediately struck his wife's lover, knocking him off the stool. His head struck the bar top and he was killed. After his death a friend of his who was a local poet composed the following rhyme:

The Cursed Stool

Look close upon this cursed stool,
And you will see
The deep dark stain that
Once was me.
For I was killed
Afore my time
My manhood cut whilst in its prime.
So cursed be them
Who'd sit upon this stool,
Be they wise-man or be they fool,
And in a dream your fate will see
That death will follow on day three.

Rumour has it that ever since then anyone else sitting on the stool by the bar either died shortly afterwards or was taken ill. Afterwards four people died after sitting on this stool. The good news is this has not happened for a long time for the cursed stool has now been destroyed or lost so customers are now safe from the curse of the Angel. The lay preacher divorced his wife and she later married a gardener while Albert's family were put into the workhouse. It is not known if the lay preacher was hung for murder.

The Angel remains one of Witney's most popular pubs but also one of its smallest. It serves reasonably priced food during the day and in the winter has an open fire. However during the evenings at the weekend all the seats and tables are removed to cater for the younger trade. The Angel is well known for its very attractive floral displays and hanging baskets. The 18th century bow windows have a preservation order on them.

BUTCHER'S ARMS (Map V) Corn Street.

This was never a butcher's shop although there used to be one across the road at No: 79 so it is possible a previous owner once owned both. Originally two 18th century single storey cottages with perhaps thatched roofs it was later enlarged with a second floor. This can be clearly seen by the different stone work between the two levels.

It is possible that a tewry (alleyway) divided the cottages in the middle, for the small pool room has a window and two door gaps, all with two feet thick stone work. Perhaps this room was once the kitchen of one of the cottages.

Previously a free house reopened in 1973, it was sold to Enterprise Inns in 2005 with a new tenant. One bar to the left of the entrance where real ales are sold with also a large display of other beers, wines and spirits, some of which cannot be found elsewhere in Witney. It also has a large private room at the rear, formerly a barn, which is available for private functions, and a small, secluded garden beyond that. Sky TV with sports channels and posters depicting pubs and their prices in previous centuries. Now smoking is not allowed smokers can sit outside on wood seats or in the pleasant garden. Not normally open until 2.30pm except at weekends.

CARPENTER'S ARMS (Map F) Newland

Formerly a Morrell's pub when it opened in 1822 it was originally two 18th century cottages built with the local Cotswold stone with black oak beams. A carpenter owned one of the cottages with his workshop at the rear, hence the name. Carpentry and joinery was a common trade in Newland then.

Nearby was the warehouse of Charles Early's blanket mill and he would often surprise his workers on night shift with beer and sausages and mash supplied by this pub. Also the Cogges Vestry used to hold their meetings here.

A more recent publican was fond of his own drink and when he got drunk would often lock the door with customers still inside and refuse to open it - sometimes not until two in the morning. The pub has an attractive garden to the rear and a large car park.

CHEQUERS (Map T) Corn Street

Yet another pub recently bought by Enterprise Inns, an 18th century building with a front extension built on at a later date. Former owners, John and Janet Coleman used to have the Nag's Head, also in Corn Street which was famous for its rustic bar. When that closed in 1989 they left to run a bar in Spain for a while taking their bar with them. On their return to Witney, John, a former London taxi driver, at his own considerable expense re-imported his bar and installed it in his new pub. The bar is still there. He also carried out considerable alterations to the pub, most of it by himself,

opening up a much larger room to the side. During these alterations he found a Witney monetary token hidden in a fireplace. The pub now caters for the younger trade with late night closing at the weekends with entertainment and Sky sports. It has a small garden at the rear with wooden gates that lead into The Crofts and a view of the Wychwood Brewery.

COURT INN (Map D) Bridge Street (Old Court Hotel)

As the name suggests this pub was also a hotel but it was never a coaching inn. Payne's horse bus and carriers who ran a regular service from here to Witney Station and back during the late 19th century once used the stables to the side of the building through the tewry. The same horses also pulled the local fire engine. At one time the local court used to meet in the Staple Hall opposite but later moved to a purpose built court-room next door and this pub was named after it.

Both lawyers and their clients used this pub, which must have made some interesting conversations at times. At one time the sign was two lawyers in black silhouette. One landlord, some time ago it must be said got into financial difficulties, stole the takings for the week, then borrowed a car from a local dealer.

He phoned him up from Heathrow to tell him his car was in the long-stay car park, but he himself was off to Spain. He was never seen again, but the dealer was able to retrieve his car. This hotel has been completely refurbished lately, renamed, with entertainment and late night closing at weekends and a car park at the rear through the tewry.

CROSS KEYS (Map I) Market Square

There are two possible reasons for the name of this pub, which may have been called the Mitre or Salutation in the past. The first is the obvious connection with the bishops of Winchester to Witney. The cross keys was the emblem of St. Peter and that of an abbot.

Indeed until recently its pub sign featured St Peter with crossed keys. The second reason is a bit more obscure. The present building may be on the site of Witney's old jail. So the sign could represent jail keys.

Jails in those days were depressing places (as they probably are now) where inmates were left alone for weeks on end, made to sleep on stone floors with no toilet facilities and often the only way out was to pay for your release. Unfortunately one pauper girl was not in a position to do that for she was heavily pregnant at the time of her imprisonment and gave birth in her cell. The child was still-born and the girl bled to death. It is rumoured that she still haunts the pub.

Until 1939 the Cross Keys was a small hotel for 'commercial gentlemen' - travelling salesmen. The main building is probably 18th century made out of the local Cotswold stone with an extension built on the front at a later date. Like many old Witney buildings the pub has a tewry at the side. A Witney tewry is actually an alleyway to enable goods to be delivered to the rear of a building.

Brakspear's beers were originally brewed in this pub until the landlord moved to Henley to start his brewery there. In 2004 the brewery was sold for housing development and Witney's Wychwood Brewery bought all the brewing equipment and reinstalled it on their enlarged site in The Crofts. So in a way Brakspear's unique double-drop beers are returning home.

Formerly a Clinch's pub it has recently undergone a complete refurbishment and for a while changed its name to Ye Olde Cross Keys. It is quite dark inside, the only natural light coming from the front windows. Serves wholesome food at reasonable prices - often two for the price of one.

EAGLE TAVERN (Map Q) Corn Street

Previously a Hunt Edmunds' pub - their plaque is still on the wall outside - it became a free house under the ownership of Gordon Rollins. At that time the pub was very small with only one room with a bar. This was so small that if three people stood at it there was no room for anyone else. It did have another room opposite but it had no bar so no-one ever used it. It also had a small courtyard with outside toilets. It was, naturally, a real ale pub and certainly no food. Consequently it was a pub favoured by the older generation. One of Witney's oldest pubs for in December 1904 a Corn Street woman stole from this pub a bottle of brandy, a bottle of rum, one bottle of whisky and two bottles of gin. All to the value of 16/-! She was caught and fined £1 with a fortnight to pay.

When Gordon Rollins retired as Oxfordshire's longest serving licensee - he was in the Eagle Tavern for thirty years - the pub closed for a while until he sold it to Hook Norton Brewery. They took on a major refurbishment, walls were knocked down to

R. Gilibrand

make the pub more open plan, the bar was moved and the courtyard covered over to make an extra room. Serves meals at lunchtime. The pub still has a Victorian feel to it and naturally still serves real ale.

EAGLE VAULTS (Map M) Market Square

Another former Hunt Edmunds' pub but it is believed they had a small brewery in the cellars hence the name, the Vaults. This was once a two bar pub with the lounge to the left - known as Betty's Bar and the public bar on the right. It also had a room set aside for children where soft drinks, ice cream and teas were served. The tenant then was Ted Trowbridge but when he retired to run a small hotel on the Isle of Wight the pub was

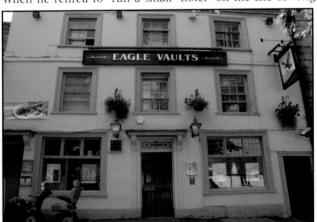

closed for refurbishment to turn it into what was then Witney's largest pub. Walls were knocked down, the shop next door was purchased and the children's area incorporated into the design. A covered patio was built and the large garden made into a popular beer garden. A former tenant was convinced the pub was haunted in Betty's Bar. He believed that in the Civil War a group of Cavaliers escaping from the Roundheads hid in a tunnel that went from this pub to the town hall opposite. They were discovered and killed, their bodies left to rot in the tunnel. At night the tenant swore he could hear noises coming from under the floorboards. However the story must be taken with a pinch of salt. It is highly unlikely that the building was a pub or tavern in those days, although there probably was a building on the site and certainly the present town hall was not built then. What he probably heard were mice under the floorboards.

Now owned by Mitchell and Butler the pub has a different clientele during the day and the evening. Lunchtimes are mainly for the older generation and meals. But after eight in the evening and six on Saturday and Sunday everything changes. The food stops and the pub is taken over by the younger people of Witney. It has Sky TV showing mainly football and music channels.

The garden now has parasols covering every table. During the summer regular barbecues are also held in the garden where smoking is allowed throughout.

In an internet poll organised by Fox FM Radio in November 2005 the Eagle Vaults was voted the best pub in Oxfordshire. In January 2006 further improvements were made with new toilets and full disabled access. Perhaps the most innovative change was the installation of a giant outdoor, all weather television screen on the wall facing the garden. Along with a large marquee with a projected screen this enabled customers to watch the World Cup - cricket matches and other sports from the garden. Currently serves breakfast from 9am then open all day. Has a car park at the rear reached via Marlborough Lane.

ELM TREE (Map C) West End

At one time there may have been an elm tree outside this pub, hence the name. Situated in one of Witney's prettiest streets with all the buildings 18th or 19th century, this pub is probably the same age. The outside of this pub is deceptive being quite large inside, its single bar serving all rooms.

It has a wide selection of clients but in the main they live locally. It has a pleasant garden to the rear but there are problems with parking as it is in a residential road.

Avoid the industrial estate at the back as this is always busy with lorries

coming and going (as well as abandoned cars). During alterations a large inglenook fireplace was uncovered.

FAT LIL'S (Map Z) 64a Corn Street.

Until 2005 this was known as Bee's Pool Club and owned by Steven Hayward a local county councillor and former mayor of Witney. A former furniture store called Bee's (hence its original name) pool was mainly played here. Although it did have a full licence it mainly catered for the younger trade. It later became Q Pool Club.

Now Witney's newest pub it opened in January 2007 and has been extensively refurbished as an entertainment bar with a large stage. Only open in the evenings except on Sunday when it opens at noon, with late night closing at weekends. An admission charge is usually made.

FLEECE (Map O) Church Green

Previously called the Marlborough Head or Duke's Head this large inn regularly features in the best pub guide and overlooks Church Green and St. Mary's Church with its steeple modelled on Christ Church Cathedral in

Oxford, it was here that Clinch's brewery started in 1811. John Clinch leased the pub and started brewing ales in an outhouse - many publicans did that during this period. By 1830 his brewing business was expanding so fast he had to find new premises. He found them over the road, knocked down a few houses and built his new brewery there. More details of Clinch's Brewery can be found in Chapter Four.

Dylan Thomas, when he lived at South Leigh between 1948-49 was a frequent visitor to this inn. He would cycle from his caravan in the Manor House grounds stopping off in the Fleece for a pint - actually several pints! While in there he would recite his poems to the locals before carefully climbing on his bike to wobble back to South Leigh. A less welcome 'artist' was a tramp who offered to paint a picture of the pub in July 1906. He was drunk, and the landlord told him to get out and then ejected him. The tramp was arrested and pleaded guilty in court on a drunk and disorderly charge and was sent to prison for seven days.

GRIFFIN (Map G)   Newland

The last pub out of Witney on the Oxford road it opened in 1786. Formerly a Garne of Burford pub, when Wadworths of Devizes acquired that brewery in 1969 this pub came into their ownership. It is their only pub in Witney.

Opposite during the 18th century and the days of the stagecoach, stood a tollgate and one fateful day the driver of a coach lost his reins at Barnard Gate where the road makes a long descent into Witney. He lost control of his team and as it approached Witney it crashed into the tollgate killing several passengers. Horses for watering and topping-up steam engines used the brook that runs along side it. In the past it has also flooded the pub. The pub has a regular clientele from the locals who live in the area.

HOLLYBUSH (Map S) Corn Street

One of Witney's oldest pubs with records going back to 1603 when it was probably a tailor's shop. The local Witney to Burford post chaise stopped at this pub to take on post and passengers until the middle of the 19th century.

Believed to be haunted by the ghost of a previous landlord who committed suicide after getting into debt. The barn to the rear was converted into a rock venue called The Pit. Many local bands have played their first gigs in this hall. Now under new management it is gaining a reputation for its food.

HOUSE OF WINDSOR (Map B) West End

This attractive pub has had several different names in the past. At the turn of the 20th century it was called the Czar of Russia and on the outbreak of the war, the King of Prussia, a very unfortunate name while we were at war with Germany. Taking the lead from the Royal Family in 1917, who had German surnames, it changed to the House of Windsor.

Has a good reputation for its food with large garden at the rear. See also Nelson in the past-pub's chapter. There were plans to change this pub into a private house but they were turned down by the planning committee.

IZI (Map K) Market Square

Witney's largest pub it was originally called Hush Bar when it opened 7 November 2001. Unfortunately this was also the name for a chain of bars elsewhere and they were forced into a name change. Not perhaps a pub in the strictest sense of the word but a bistro type bar with the younger generation in mind. It has full air-conditioning, flat screen televisions, with comfortable armchairs and settees as well as normal tables and chairs. Disabled toilets are available on the ground floor and in the summer months the large windows open up fully with an attractive border of

R. Gilbrand

boxed flowers giving the impression of drinking and eating outside. Serves good wholesome food and a variety of drinks. The bar is unusual in that it is chest high even for normal people with staff able to look down on them. However this does stop people crowding the bar.

Open late with a night club on the second floor which was opened on Thursday 24th November 2005.

MARLBOROUGH HOTEL (Map L) Market Square

Central Witney's largest hotel, it is a former coaching inn and was previously called the Blue Boar but when the Churchill family took over the town from the bishops of Winchester it changed its name. Probably because the tenant at that time may have been a former servant of the family and financed by them.

The Marlborough has always been the traditional meeting place for Witney business people. It was in this hotel that Charles Early, Henry Akers, Joseph Druce, William Payne and Malachi Bartlett, with help from Clinch's Bank, formed the Witney Railway Company in 1859. The railway connected Fairford, Bampton, Witney and Yarnton with Oxford where connections could be made to London, Worcester and Wolverhampton. The company, which still held its board meetings in the hotel, lasted for 31 years until 1890 when they sold out to the Great Western.

It is unlikely that any stagecoaches entered the yard through the small low tewry at the side as they would have been too high and they probably reached the stables via Marlborough Lane from Corn Street. However a post chaise would have found it easy. The stables have since been converted into bedrooms. The Marlborough is often called the centre of the town and by tradition, following in the wake of the stagecoaches, all buses still stop outside.

Recent refurbishment altered the main bar into a brasserie with a restaurant at the rear. During this restoration a Charles I iron fire back was uncovered with the king's coat of arms. This is now on display in the fireplace in the bar although it is probably a Victorian fake as it is highly unlikely Charles ever visited or stayed at the inn.

As a hotel it serves meals throughout the day and evenings and has a large car park.

NEW INN (Map W) Corn Street
This pub has had a chequered life since it opened in the 1860s as a hostel for the navvies who helped build the Witney railway. It has closed several times in the last ten years, but the present licensee has revived it by making it into a real ale pub. It was elected CAMRA Oxfordshire pub of the year in 2005. It also holds the Cask Marque for the quality of its beers.

Always has a good selection of beers, some of which only real ale fanatics have ever heard of. Opening hours vary during weekdays with the occasional entertainment during the evening.

Always supports most national charity events, like BBC Children In Need. Has one large L-shaped bar with a flat screen TV showing live sport. Has a small garden to the rear and is the last pub going out of Witney through Corn Street.

NORTON'S (Map J)   Langdale Court

When the Woolgate Centre was built towards the end of the 1980s this was Witney's first café-bar then known as Raffles. Unusual in its design the bar to the left of the main door was actually on a stage with the restaurant to the right. It also had a room upstairs. Later it changed its name and has been completely refurbished since. Very popular with the youth of Witney and now has a late licence.

R. Gilbrand

29

OLD COURT HOTEL (See Court Inn)

PLOUGH (Map H) High Street

This charming pub is possibly one of Witney's oldest with a building on this site since at least 1606 when it may have been a weaver's cottage. Certainly next door John Butler ran a pub until 1720 when the master blanket makers built their Blanket Hall. Butler was also a weaver so this building may have been his private residence.

Although it looks large from the outside it only has two small rooms, the bar area having an open fireplace. In a complete 24/7 no parking zone with no private parking facilities, and situated in the 'dead' area of Witney for the licensed trade makes it extremely difficult to make this a profitable pub and many have failed. Consequently this pub has had a chequered life of late.

Now owned by Admiral Taverns and under new tenancy it seems to have taken on a new lease of life. In 1840 it belonged to John Clinch the Witney brewer with Thomas Collier his tenant when it was called the Plough and Shuttle. In 1962 it was owned by Courage after they had bought out the Clinch brewery. The Plough is unique as it has Witney's only pub riverside garden, which is known as the secret garden. The hall to the rear, up steep stone steps was once the brewhouse for the Blanket Hall Brewery and in the past has been used as a clubroom, a restaurant and is now called the Loom Room where local bands play. There are plans to turn the room beneath it, currently used as a storeroom into a restaurant. This pub was severely hit by the floods of July 2007.

RED LION HOTEL (Map R) Corn Street

R. Gilibrand

Formerly a Morrell's pub it was taken over by Greene King when they took over Morrell's of Oxford. Built in the 19th century it has two large bars and may have been a small coaching inn or posting house in the past. It has a tewry to the side with a small covered garden. At the rear was a room, called The Barn where pop and jazz music was played on a regular basis.

Its longest serving tenant was W. Broadbent who was there between December 1963 to August 1984. Has recently undergone a complete refurbishment.

ROBIN HOOD (Map A) Hailey Road

One of Witney's newest pubs although it does stand on the site of a former Robin Hood. The current licensee's lounge was once the public bar. A pub that serves the various estates in the area it has two bars with entertainment. It also has a very large garden to the rear up a flight of steps.

ROWING MACHINE (Map X) Windrush Valley Road.

Originally a Whitbread pub when it was built in the 1960s, it was then leased out to Morrells. Its name comes from a machine employed at Early's mill and driven by a donkey and was suggested by Richard Early. In 1999 it changed its name to the Flying Machine, possibly because the estate before it was built was used by de Havilland during the last war to repair fighter aircraft.

This change of name upset quite a few of the locals, some even appearing on *Central News* to voice their views. Fortunately there was a change of opinion and it has since reverted back to its original name.

A large pub with two bars, one of which has Sky TV showing sport, has a dart board and pool table. The lounge bar has a separate bar while its most popular feature in the summer is its large garden with a children's area and an Aunt Sally pitch.

ROYAL OAK (Map N) High Street

One of Witney's oldest buildings built in about 1609 but it is not thought it has always been a pub, possibly a group of cottages down a tewry. Now a freehouse that serves the local Wychwood beers.

Part of the courtyard has since been converted into a covered area with glass doors, although part of the garden still remains.

A very popular pub during lunchtimes when it serves excellent food. Now has one main bar with its bar in the middle. Previously it had two rooms, with a bar in the middle, but to get from one bar to the other customers had to go outside.

Two former bank employees who took on the licence of this pub were very fond of playing practical jokes on their customers. One stool at the bar had a hidden turn screw beneath it. Anyone sitting on this stool who was called away on nature's business would, on their return found

themselves a little higher than before, until finally the stool would be so high it would be impossible to climb on to it.

Another regular also happened to be the butcher at the nearby supermarket. Returning from the Brewsters' Session at the local Court House, both licensees, dressed in smart suits, entered the supermarket and making out they were plainclothes police demanded to see the butcher. When the butcher appeared he was grabbed by his arms and frog marched out of the shop, his 'captors' telling every one he was a dangerous criminal and that he was under arrest. They took him back to their pub where they locked him in and demanded money for his release to be paid to a local charity. The supermarket paid up and fortunately took the episode in good faith while the two licensees were not arrested themselves for impersonating police officers.

THREE HORSESHOES (Map U) Corn Street

This 18th century building was once the property of Morland of Abingdon but is now part of the Greene King chain of pubs. Possibly originally a group of weavers cottages with a blacksmith's nearby. When Holloway Road was built in the 1950s one of the cottages was pulled down.

More of a restaurant now than a pub although it does have a small bar

33

to the left of the entrance. Serves good English style food with the occasional fish night. Always best to book in advance, especially for Sunday lunch. It seems that even in 1906 it was well known for its meals. In January of that year the Witney Pig Association

held its 4th anniversary dinner there. The club was formed to encourage home produced pork to save money on imported pigs and that Witney should have its own pig factory.

THREE PIGEONS (Map E) Woodgreen

This pub over-looks the quiet Woodgreen and certainly dates back as a pub since 1783 when on Thursday July 17, John Wesley preached outside his first Witney sermon. Built in the local Cots-wold stone it has two bars and a restaurant area with a pleasant

34

secluded garden at the rear. Also has seats outside where drinkers can enjoy the view. Was originally a group of cottages with one of them belonging to a game merchant - hence its name. At one time a coach full of regulars from a London pub on a day trip paid a visit to the pub and on seeing the large green outside, enjoyed themselves by playing a game of cricket. This soon became an annual event with the two pub sides playing friendly matches.

WINDRUSH INN (Map Y) Burford Road

Built by Ind Coope to their typical post war design to act as a road house on the A40 to Cheltenham just after the last war. It was a very popular pub for race-goers to the various meetings held on that course. That was until the Witney by-pass was built which took away much of its trade. So much

so that a previous landlord would, on race days, post signboards on the round-about where the by-pass joins the A40, directing customers to his pub.

One set of customers did find their way, the famous

Beatles stopped off for a meal here and the pub was shut to give them some privacy. However some of the local girls soon discovered this and surrounded the inn. Another frequent visitor was David (Del Boy) Jason who has relatives living in the area.

This pub has two bars, an old fashioned public bar where darts and pool can be played, and a large saloon area. The restaurant has also been enlarged and this looks out onto the pub's very large garden with play equipment for children, while in the distance is one of the best views in Witney. It has an uninterrupted view of the whole Windrush valley with the Cotswold Hills in the distance.

Map of Past Witney Pubs
KEY
A Early's Mill; **B** Hudson's Brewery; **C** Smith's Mill; **D** Fire St.; **E** Blanket Hall Brewery;
F Union Workhouse; **G** Post Office; **H** Britannia Brewery; **I** Town Hall; **J** Buttercross;
K Clinch's Brewery; **L** Walker's Mill; **M** Farm Mill; **N** Police Station

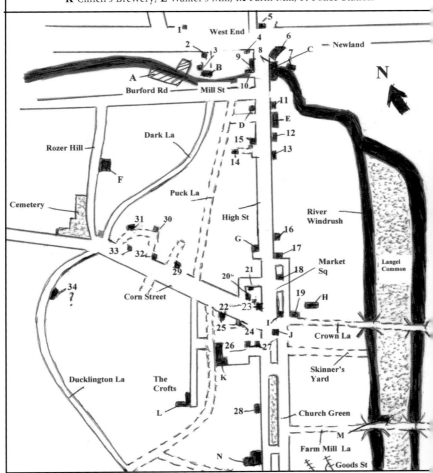

CHAPTER THREE

Past Witney Pubs and Inns

At a time when there was no TV, radio, or organised entertainment outside the church, pubs in Witney, like elsewhere, were the only places the average man could go outside working hours. And in Witney that need was well fulfilled.

It has not been easy to find some of these long lost pubs, some having been pulled down, redeveloped into shops and offices or converted into houses. Newland and Cogges which are now part of Witney on the Oxford road were, at one time separate villages. From records it seemed that they were extremely fond of their ale as well as a certain rivalry between the Witney people and the villagers.

The first record of any pub in this area was the Hare and Hounds in 1730, but obviously there were alehouses long before that. Within 50 years the villages could boast six pubs all competing for the same trade. They were the Star, the Crown, the Axe, the George, the Swan and the Plasterer's Arms. Unfortunately these same records do not tell us where they were. Also at that time the Griffin opened in 1789 opposite the Newland Turnpike and the Carpenters' Arms in 1822, both of which still exist. Other pubs where records have been lost were, the Dolphin, the Golden Balls, the Gibbet Head, the Wheatsheaf, the Clothmaker's Arms, the Tallow Chandler's Arms and the Talbot all at one time in Witney.

All illustrations in this section although based on research may not be accurate representations.

ANCHOR (Map 10) Bridge Street.
Unfortunately very little is known about this pub except it is known that it was on the banks of the River Windrush on the north side of the bridge. The present site is a sports car showroom.

AXE
All records of this pub lost but thought to have been in Newland

BELL   (Map 25) 57, Corn Street.
This pub was one of the casualties of the loss in trade after World War I. When the tenant - or owner - left it must have been very sudden for

he simply shut and locked the door and walked away, leaving this pub as a time capsule of what pubs in the 1920s looked like.

Inside the original bar and fittings remained with bottles of beer gathering dust and cobwebs on shelves. It remained that way for many years and the building has now been converted into housing for older residents by the Acorn Trust. It was in this area that Witney first developed and it is believed a monastery once existed around here. It is possible that this pub was named after the monk's bell tower.

BLACK'S HEAD See Black Moor

BLACK HORSE (Map 1) 72 West End
This pub was closed during World War 1 and it became a hostel for Belgian refugees who were then fleeing the German advance in their own country. Many came to this country and Witney. Requisitioned by the Witney Urban District Council as an overflow to the Union Workhouse. After the war it became a Salvation Army hostel for down-and-outs, and needless to say was not very popular in the area. It is now a private house and externally has changed very little. Also see Weavers Arms.

BLACK MOOR (Map 8) Bridge Street
This pub had several names during its lifetime, all named after the Crusades, including, the Saracen's Head. the Black-a-Moor, Moor's Head, Black's Head and in the 1850s the Prince Albert. Another that suffered through lack of trade during the 1920s and it was demolished and was for several years a wallpaper and paint shop. This too was demolished in 1998 and is now a house.

BLACK PRINCE See Prince of Wales

BLUE BOAR See also Marlborough

Although this building has changed over the years, this drawing (right) is still recogniseable as the present hotel.

BLACK SWAN (Map 34) Ducklington Lane.

The difficulty with this pub is finding out exactly where on the Ducklington Lane it actually was. For certain it was probably on the old lane and not the present one which was built much later. The other problem is was it actually in Ducklington Lane at all? It is possible that the Black Swan could have been the original name of the present New Inn.

BOAR'S HEAD See the Bull

BORDER OF LOVE (Map 21) Marlborough Lane.

A rather unsavoury alehouse, the type of place where women would not enter. Unfortunately certain women did, hence the name for the pub. But this, of course could have been a nickname the local residents gave it. It was closed, one can only guess the reason why, in about 1915 and the last known landlord, Harry Wright later went on to serve in the Marlborough. Until recently it was owned by the Marlborough and was the owner's private residence. It is now a private house called Rose Cottage.

BRITANNIA   (Map 14) High Street

A very small alehouse at the end of the Dovecote in High Street. Situated down a tewry it was known to have existed in 1841 but the date of its closure is unknown. Could have been where William Gillet started the Britannia Brewery in 1860, before moving to the rear of the Corn Exchange. The building is now a private house.

BULL   (Map 27) Market Square

Formerly called the Boar's Head this pub is still fondly remembered by some older Witney residents, if only for its unbeatable darts team. It closed in the late 1950s and the building is now a suite of offices and a second hand bookshop. To the side at the entrance to the Church Green industrial estate above a door can still be seen its name engraved in the glass.

CARPENTER'S ARMS (Map 33) Corn Street

An alehouse situated down a lane off Corn Street, probably now the site of the Stagecoach garage. It was also the site of Witney's first cinema known as the 'Penny Gaff'. There is a tulip tree planted on the side of the pavement with a plaque to commemorate it. It was open between 1912 to 1914 by E.A. Huddleston. He later moved into Church Green with the Palace Cinema now the site of the Palace night club. Yet another of Witney's old alehouses that probably closed prior to 1910.

CENTRAL HOTEL   See Temperance Hotel

CLOTHMAKER'S ARMS

All records of this pub have been lost, but during the author's current researches mention was made to him of a pub at the top end of Mill Street on a triangle of land in a building next to Early's Mill boiler house. What better name to give it next door to a cloth mill. However, there is no written proof and must therefore be pure speculation.

COACH AND HORSES (Map 20) Marlborough Lane

Probably an alehouse or lodging house for stagecoach drivers and persons of lesser importance after dropping off richer passengers in the Marlborough. The exact location is not known but the most obvious place is now used as a staff car park for Barclay's Bank. Not known when it closed but probably at the end of the coaching era i.e. middle of 18th century.

CROWN Newland

All records lost

CROWN HOTEL (Map 19) Market Square

This major Witney coaching inn with large stables to the rear of the building is best remembered for its association with the Chartist Movement

of the 19th century, which was formed by Fergus Edward O'Conner and was the forerunner of the British Labour party. Born in Ireland on 18 July 1796 he entered parliament in 1832 but lost his seat in 1835 then in 1838 founded the *Northern Star* newspaper. Well known for his extreme left wing politics he was imprisoned for a year in 1841 for seditious libel. On his release he founded the National Charter Association. One of his demands was a land ownership plan for ordinary workers which O'Conner based on a form of agrarian communism.

On 24 June 1847 at the Crown Hotel he bought at auction 297 acres of land at Minster Lovell for £10,678 to create a workers' village on the site, known as Charterville Allotments. He built special bungalows, each having 4 acres of ground to house these new farmers, many of whom came from the docklands and the north-east England who had no idea about farming or how to run a market garden, let alone be self-sufficient.

Not surprisingly the scheme collapsed and O'Conner was declared bankrupt. He was declared insane in 1852 and was committed to an asylum where he died on 30 August 1855. However he was well remembered by those he tried to help and over 50,000 mourners attended his funeral.

His village was sold off to the highest bidders in lots (see The Star) and it is ironic that his village has now become a highly sought after place to live. Some of the original cottages still remain but most have been replaced by large detached modern houses, still in their acres of ground. The present village, which is still know as Charterville, has a small street named after him.

The Crown Hotel was later converted in the early 20th century into offices which included the auctioneers Habgood and Mammatt and Frost the coal merchants. The southern end of the building was demolished in the late 1970s to make way for Langdale Gate and a Co-op supermarket. Since then the whole site has been once more refurbished and has branches of Argos, New Look and Richard Dyas now on the site. Fortunately much of the fascia for the top floor has remained. When the southern half was demolished the site was excavated for traces of medieval Witney but nothing of note was discovered.

CZAR OF RUSSIA See House of Windsor

DOLPHIN
All records are now lost but may have been a former or later name for the Anchor.

GEORGE See Prince of Wales

GEORGE Newland
A 17th or 18th century pub where all records have been lost.

GEORGE AND DRAGON (Map 26) Church Green
An alehouse situated in what is now an industrial estate, this pub had its own brewhouse, so that was possibly the reason John William Clinch moved from the Fleece to set up his new brewery on the site in 1830. Probably closed as a pub at that time.

GIBBET'S HEAD See Lamb and Flag

GOLDEN BALLS
All records of this pub have been lost.

HARE AND HOUNDS Newland
Nothing is known about this pub.

HARRIERS (Map 4) West End
This Hunt Edmunds' pub is fondly remembered by the older generation of Witney people. Not known when it first opened but probably closed in the early 1960s. The building is now a private house but the brewery's plaque can still be seen on the wall.

HEN AND CHICKENS (Map 22) Hen and Chickens Lane off Corn Street
To the side and rear of the pet shop and ladies dress shop in Corn Street is a narrow lane once called Hen and Chickens Lane. At the end is now a small car park but here nearly two centuries ago stood this alehouse. Many large inns during the 18th century had smaller hotel taps which served the lesser types of people and this could have served that purpose for the Lamb and Flag. Date of its demolition is unclear but probably around 1832 when the Lamb and Flag was demolished.

JOLLY TUCKER (Map 5) West End.
Situated in West End this pub was named after the tuckers who worked in the mills. In February 1904 Charles Early along with a number of clergymen and local citizens presented a petition with 1029 names to the

Licensing Authority to reduce the number of pubs in the town, which by then was in excess of one pub to 100 of the population.

Early along with the Temperance Society considered this too many. The Bench decided to consider the matter but it was not until June 1906 the County Licensing Committee decided that the Jolly Tucker and the Malt Shovel should close down, although they did admit that both pubs were clean and well run.

Applications for compensation had to be submitted by the end of the month. In truth it was not only in Witney pubs were being closed down at this time. The Temperance lobby was very strong then and many employers, who were also magistrates, supported them as many of their workers were off sick through drunkenness. The owners of the Jolly Tucker received £1250 in compensation in January 1907, although it was highly unlikely the tenant received any for his loss in trade and home. The building is still there and is now a fish and chip takeaway and a post office, which is alleged to be haunted by a previous pub tenant's wife or daughter.

JOLLY WAGGONERS (Map 12) High Street
Very little is known about this pub which was probably used by the waggoners who brought wool to the town for use in the mills. It was believed to have been situated in what is now the entrance to Witan Way in High Street. Probably closed when the Blanket Hall closed as a meeting and inspection hall.

KING OF PRUSSIA See House of Windsor

KING'S ARMS (Map 11) High Street
The owner of this inn, John Payne left in his will dated 24 February 1821, the King's Arms, garden, stables, outbuilding, his stock in trade, plate, furniture, linen and china to his friends, John Cooper of Wheatley and John Cox of Reading. However he did instruct that his wife Joan could stay and trade on the premises until her own death or remarriage.

In 1841 Joan either died or remarried for the King's Arms was put up for auction by Cox and Cooper on December 29 at the premises. The notice advertising the sale claimed that the inn was a freehold, long established inn and commercial hotel. The site had a substantial front with a carriage entrance, commercial room, back parlour, kitchen, bar, sitting room, six letting bedrooms, and domestic offices. It also had an excellent

brewhouse, cellar, store houses, stabling for 16 horses, sheds and a large warehouse with the whole inn well supplied with water. The notice also stated that it had a good retail wine and spirit trade and that the inn ranked with commercial gentlemen as one of the most comfortable establishments in the country. The town had a large manufacturing population and good weekly markets while the consumption of beer was considerable.

The last owner was Anne Ashton who was also a seamstress. It closed in the 1950s and is now a large furniture store while the upstairs rooms are now occupied by the Windrush Club.

KING'S HEAD (Map 13) High Street
Little is known about this 19th century pub, even when it closed. The site is now an Indian restaurant.

LAMB AND FLAG   (Map 23) Market Square
During the 18th century this prestigious inn was one of Witney's major coaching inns on the London to Gloucester stagecoach route run by the Gloucester Flying Machine Stagecoach Company. A large building on the

corner of Market Square and Corn Street with stables to the rear. It had many different names in the past, including the Bear, Old Town House and also nicknamed the Long Bar by the locals.

Certainly in 1771 it was shown on a timetable for the stagecoach line as the Lamb which claimed it was 69¼ miles from Hyde Park Corner in London. Later it was called the Lamb and Flag after the crest of Witney Town which in turn signifies the Lamb of God holding a banner with the cross of St George. The inn was demolished in 1832 and wholesale grocers, Tarrant and Sons built a shop and warehouse on the site. This building was itself destroyed - allegedly by a stray rocket firework - on King George V's coronation night 20 June 1911. About fifty years later a new building was erected on the site. A building that many people disapproved of because it was out of character with the rest of the buildings in Market Square. For a while it was Ford's Electrical, a branch of the Co-op, but is now a Sue Ryder charity shop.

MALT SHOVEL　(Map 24) Corn Street

This Clinch's pub had direct access to their brewery at the rear but was closed down in 1906 by the Licensing Committee (supported by the Temperance Society) as they considered there were too many pubs in Witney (See Jolly Tucker for more details of this event). Clinch's Brewery received £761 by way of compensation. The building, which is still recognisable as a former pub, is now a television shop.

MITRE　See Cross Keys

MOOR'S HEAD　See Black's Head

NAG'S HEAD (Map 29)　Corn Street

This very popular pub was the last to close in recent times in 1989 when the owners, John and Janet Coleman left to run a bar in Spain. This pub was famous for it rustic oak bar made and installed by John - a former London taxi driver. Had a mixed clientele but mainly younger people where the poolroom at the rear was a popular feature. When John and Janet left for Spain he took his bar with him and installed it there. They returned to Witney a few years later and once more the bar was dismantled and shipped back to England. At first he was in negotiations to buy Bees Pool Club but eventually settled on the Chequers. There his bar was once more installed and it is still there, although John and Janet retired from the pub trade some time later. See also Tallow Chandler's Arms.

NELSON INN (Map 2)　West End

In May 1901 the death of George Hudson was announced. At that time he was the oldest serving landlord in the town having first acquired the licence for this pub 35 years earlier in 1866. Like many licensees in those days he also had a second job, as a butcher with his own slaughterhouse in West End. It is known that there was a slaughterhouse on the corner with Woodstook Road where cattle were led down the road from the cattle market in Market Square. He may have had an interest in Hudson's Brewery (or perhaps even started it) which was close to this pub. Not known when closed but probably shortly after his death. The site is now the entrance to the West End Industrial Estate. However there is an opinion that the Nelson was once on the site of the House of Windsor before it was called the Czar of Russia and that the original site of the Czar of Russia was in fact on the opposite side of the road

OLD TOWN ARMS   See Lamb and Flag

PLASTERER'S ARMS
Little is known about this 18th century pub except it probably was in Newland.

PRINCE OF WALES (Map 15) High Street
Previously called the Black Prince and sold at auction in 1856 at the King's Arms it was then called the George. Built in 1703 the original building was of poor quality the internal walls made of wattle and daub (straw and

mud) it has been first a Rover then a Ford car showroom and garage for many years. On its last evening before it was converted the new owner held a private party for his staff, but during the evening several gatecrashers entered thinking it was opened again as a pub. There were plans to turn the large car storage area into housing but the old pub now has a preservation order on it although on the ground floor very little of it remains externally.

QUEEN'S HEAD (Map 16) 10. High Street
Little is known about this pub but it was probably named after Queen Anne who gave the master blanket makers their charter. The site is now a shoe shop.

ROCKET TAVERN (Map 31) Corn Street
Little is known about this pub except it was nowhere near the railway or the local station, possibly at the bottom end of Corn Street. In 1840 this could have been a previous name for the Star. Star being a general name for the various locomotives that worked the Witney rail line.

ROEBUCK (Map 30) Corn Street
Yet another Corn Street or even in West End, where all records have been lost.

ROSEDEAN HOTEL (Map 28) Church Green
It is not certain if this hotel ever had a licence but as it was owned by Tom Forshew, the managing director of Clinch's Brewery it probably had. He sold the hotel to the Urban District Council in 1936 and they used it until recently as offices for their housing department. It has now been converted into flats and affordable housing.

SALUTATION See Cross Keys.

SARACEN'S HEAD See Black Moor.

STAPLE HALL (Map 6) Corner of Bridge Street and Newland
This former inn was built on the site of a 13th century wool warehouse and during the 16th century it became a refuge for students from Trinity

College, Oxford escaping the plague. After a major fire in the 17th century it was completely rebuilt. It was founded as an inn by William Townsend and his wife Ursula Marriott in 1668. Ursula lived throughout the 17th century and into the 18th and on her 100th birthday attended the christening of her 100th offspring.

Apart from its coaching connections - this inn was also on the London to Gloucester route - it was also a favourite meeting place for the master blanket makers to meet before they built the Blanket Hall. It closed as an inn during the 19th century and in turn became a Post Office, a Congregational Church and a courthouse.

Staple Hall is reputed to be haunted on the top floor by the ghost of a very beautiful young lady. Dressed in a long ball gown and wearing a diamond necklace, she walks through what was called the blue room. During the 1940s guests attending weekend parties held by the then resident, the Registrar of Witney used to play a game called Hunt the Ghost. Often they heard footsteps approaching a bedroom door but when they opened it no-one was there. The building is now a residential home for the elderly.

STAR (Map 32) Corn Street
A pub still remembered with affection by some older residents but not by the original inhabitants of Charterville Allotments. When Fergus O'Conner went bankrupt their homes were sold off in this pub to the highest bidders. Now homeless and away from their roots in London they staged a riot outside this pub. It is now a Chinese takeaway and may have been called the Waggon and Horses in the past and The Rocket in 1840.

STAR
Yet another Newland pub of which little is known.

SUNDIAL (Map 18) Market Square.
A late 19th century pub that later became a chemist's shop, a greengrocers' and is now a branch of the Oxford charity Oxfam. Outside this shop once stood the Witney Elm, on which the locals used to post notices of forthcoming events etc. Unfortunately it was infected with Dutch elm disease in the 1970s and had to be removed. As it was so popular as an information board the council placed a purpose-built one at the entrance to the Woolgate Centre.

SWAN
Believed to have been at Newland during the 18th century.

TALBOT
All records of this pub have been completely lost.

TALLOW CHANDLER'S ARMS
In 1734 there was a major fire that started in a candle makers' workshop down a tewry off Corn Street which also destroyed thirty other properties. On the corner of this tewry was a pub which was later better known as the Nag's Head. Although it is speculation this pub's original name could have been the Tallow Chandler's Arms and the second business of the candle maker. However other opinions place this pub on Church Green.

TEMPERANCE HOTEL (Map 17) Market Square

This alcohol-free pub was originally called the Coffee Tavern when it was set up by the master blanket makers and the Temperance Society in 1879 who sold shares to the general public. However the idea that thirsty working men would prefer a cup of coffee instead of their traditional pint of bitter never worked. But strangely it was a favourite place for the Tucker's Annual Feast, although as this was organised and paid for by their employers per- haps not. It never real- ly caught on as an alco- hol free pub, plus it was very badly organised and was soon in financial difficulties. It was not until 1903 that it showed a profit and then only £27 for the whole year. Later it changed its name to the Temperance Hotel and let out rooms to travellers then later to the Central Hotel. It is now a large Boots store, however parts of the hotel can still be seen in the non-public areas and one member of staff believes it to be haunted.

UNION (Map 3) West End
Possibly the brewery tap for the little known Hudson's Brewery. The area is now an industrial estate.

WAGGON AND HORSES See the Star

WEAVER'S ARMS
Not on map because all records of this West End pub have been lost. However what is known is that Charles Early (1824-1912) did have a workshop in West End at the Hailey Road end. There he had installed looms to produce high quality cloth. Perhaps this pub eventually became the Black Horse, although that is speculation.

WHEATSHEAF
No record of this pub in archives only hearsay.

WHITE HART (Map 7) Bridge Street
This prestigious inn existed on the banks of the River Windrush at least from the 16th century until 1841 when it appeared on a tithe map. For centuries it was Witney's premiere inn. Queen Elizabeth I stayed here on 16 September 1592 and gave the inn a tapestry which was then displayed on a wall. Unfortunately it was either lost, destroyed or stolen shortly afterwards. Another royal also stayed at this inn for when Charles I passed through Witney between 18-20 June 1644 he lodged in this inn. Perhaps the most memorable event in this inn happened on 3 February 1652. A troupe of travelling actors staged a play in an upstairs room, but at 8 pm a supporting beam gave way, sending actors and some of the audience crashing to the floor below. Five were killed and many more injured. After restoration the inn became a coaching and posting house for the *Magnet*, *Paul Pry* and *Aurors* stagecoach lines.

This area of Witney is reported to be very haunted. The bridge is haunted by a novice monk who was thrown into the river by rioters and the events of 1652 have been re-enacted several times. In 1823, John Hudson from Gloucester who was visiting relatives in the town, was walking by the site when he saw "a terrible accident unfolding before my eyes and there were loud cries of help, children screaming and the pathway was covered in dust". As he got nearer the vision vanished. The last record of the event was in 1982 when once more the vision was seen, this time on 3 February, the 330th anniversary of the accident!

In 1846 William Smith took over the brewhouse to form the White Hart Brewery and the site eventually became Smith's mill. See White Hart Brewery for more details.

WHITE LION (Map 9) Bridge Street

This little known pub was situated next to the Court Inn and parts of their stables belonged to this pub. Not known when it opened or closed as a pub but it was trading in 1841 when it paid a tithe tax of 1/4d. The building still exists and is now a private house.

CHAPTER FOUR

Witney Breweries Past and Present

One of the three Bs of Witney was beer and its brewing. Many landlords of pubs actually brewed their ales on the premises and some found that by doing so they actually made more money that way than running their pubs. Clinch's and Brakspear breweries started that way, both in Witney. Brakspear's beers were first brewed in the Cross Keys in Market Square before he moved to Henley on Thames, while John William Clinch started his brewery in the Fleece Inn on Church Green. The only remaining brewery now in Witney is the Wychwood Brewery in the Crofts which is now owned by Refresh UK.

The brewing of beer is a fine art and it is rigorously controlled at every stage of production with penalties imposed on the brewer for lack of hygiene and quality, Customs and Excise can, and do, enter a brewery without the brewery's permission. While there the inspector inspects the quality, ABV and the records of every brew made. These records must be kept up to date every day and there are heavy fines for the brewer who forgets. As the brewery is also a factory it is also subject to the health and safety laws, the many food preparation guidelines, EC rules, transport regulations as well as training staff. The life of a brewer is not an easy one but it does have its rewards. Particularly when a new brew has to be sampled.

THE WYCHWOOD BREWERY

The Eagle Maltings, Unit 10-12 Eagle Industrial Estate, The Crofts, Witney, Oxon OX28 4DP, telephone 01993 890800, Fax 01993 772553. (Photos see front and back cover)
Website: **www.wychwood.co.uk** e-mail: **intray@wychwood.co.uk**

The original brewery was started by Paddy Glenny, who was trained as a brewer in Germany, at his home in Freeland as a hobby, making beer for his own and friends' use. So popular did they become that Paddy acquired a brewing licence and in 1983 moved to the cellar of the old Eagle maltings house of Clinch's Brewery. At first he called it the Eagle Brewery but soon changed it to Glenny Brewery. In 1985 he took on a partner, Chris Moss and in 1987 they moved to Station Lane Industrial Estate making only 800 barrels a year, sold mainly to local free houses.

In 1988 they were asked to produce a special beer for the wedding of a local landlord's daughter. Chris Moss presented the guests with a delicious, dark, rich brew which became the brewery's famous Hobgoblin Ale. When Paddy Glenny left in 1992 Chris Moss took on a new partner, Ian Rogers and the brewery was renamed The Wychwood Brewery, after the medieval forest which once surrounded Witney. In 1994 the site on Station Lane had become too small, so Chris and Ian moved back to the Eagle site where they could and did produce 12,000 barrels a year. This not only included Hobgoblin but Witney Bitter and Wychwood Best. Within two years, in 1996 the first Hobgoblin beer in bottles was sold, which gave the company access to supermarkets. At the same time with help from venture capital, they started to buy their own pubs, all with the name The Hobgoblinn.

In 1997 the Wychwood Brewery was producing 30,000 barrels a year, which included many limited edition and celebratory ales with distinctive artwork and imaginative names, like Dogs Bollocks, Shire, Thirsty's, Fiddler's Elbow and Black Wych Stout.

In 2002 Chris Moss died and Ian Rogers sold the business to Refresh UK. Their 40 pubs were sold off, although they continued to use the Hobgoblinn branding under their new owners, to enable Refresh UK to concentrate solely on brewing.

In October of 2002 the Henley on Thames Brewery of Brakspear was closed and Wychwood committed themselves to bringing their famous brews back to Witney. After major building work which started in December 2003 the site was considerable enlarged to house Brakspear's brewhouse and fermenting equipment, much of it coming by road from Henley.

Apart from the Brakspear beers, Wychwood still produce Hobgoblin, celebration ales, seasonal cask ales, and a range of bottled beers which include WychCraft, Goliath, Fiddler's Elbow and Black Wych stout. In addition they produce two exclusive beers for Sainsburys and three organic beers brewed for Duchy Originals. In October 2007, Prince Charles visited the brewery.

CLINCH'S BREWERY

The most famous of Witney's breweries was that of Clinch on Church Green. Founded by John William Clinch, the son of a banker, he first started brewing in the Fleece Inn in 1811. So popular did his brew become that in 1839 he purchased several cottages on Church Green, and possibly the George and Dragon pub, demolished them and built a new brewery on the site.

Clinch did not have the advantage of running water on the site with which to brew his ales and run the machinery, but not too far away was the River Windrush with a well down Skinner's Yard. So Clinch dug a pipeline to this well and pumped the water up from there and stored it in a giant tank on the site.

In 1871 John William died and he was succeeded by his son William until his own death in 1891. A year later the brewery was formed into a limited company. At first the company was very successful buying up 70 pubs in Witney, Oxford, Swindon and even supplied beers as far away as Birmingham and to Oxford colleges. However, with the government restriction on brewing and shorter opening hours during World War I the company struggled and was only kept going with the help of Clinch's Bank. After the war the company appointed L.B. Clark as head brewer to replace John Welch and between 1929 -1939 he won sixteen first prizes, two championship gold medals, seven second prizes and ten third prizes for his beers at the annual competition organised at the Brewers Exhibition in London. Clark was probably one of the best, if not the best brewer in the country who was a Diploma Member of the Institute of Brewing. In 1939 the company owned fourteen pubs in Witney. They were, the Three Horseshoes, the Hollybush, the Nag's Head and the Star (both now closed), all in Corn Street. They also owned the Angel, the Bull (now closed), and the Cross Keys in Market Square. The Carpenter's Arms at Newland and the Three Pigeons on Woodgreen, the King's Arm's and the Prince of Wales in High Street (both now closed) the Royal Oak, and the Plough also in the High Street as well as their original pub the Fleece on Church Green. Tom Forshew, the managing director between the wars also privately owned the Rosedean Hotel on Church Green, but sold this to the District Council as offices for £2,000 in 1936. Tom Forshew was related to the Clinch family by marriage, however after his son was killed during the Second World War he lost interest in the company.

A post war boom in sales after the war helped a little but the company still had to find more capital which was found in 1949, but this took away the family's control. By the nineteen-sixties with competition from much larger breweries and the decline in real ales in favour of the continental lagers, the company was in deep financial trouble. It was only by selling off some of their pubs and loans from the bank that kept them afloat.

In 1962 an approach was made from Courage Brewery to buy them out and the offer of £850,000 was accepted. As expected the brewery was closed down a year later although it remained a local distribution depot for some time afterwards. The site is now a small industrial estate.

THE BLANKET HALL BREWERY

In 1844 the master blanket makers of Witney decided that they had no further need of their meeting hall in the High Street. One of their members, Edward Early put in a bid of £200 for the premises and it was accepted. He had been looking for suitable premises as a brewery for some time and the site was ideal, it even had a brewhouse at the rear.

Edward set up his son Joseph in partnership with William Smith as brewers. Not sure if the partnership would work he only gave them yearly leases and he was proved right, for within two years William had left to form his own brewery. Joseph remained on his own until 1869 when he sold up to the Shillingford brothers. They expanded the business before selling up to Arthur Bateman. In 1890 he in turn sold out to Clinch's Brewery and they closed the brewery down. Bateman died shortly after. Many businesses occupied the site from then on, including a mineral water factory. It is now a private house which still has its unusual one-hand clock at the top of the building.

THE WHITE HART BREWERY

Founded by William Smith after he left the Blanket Hall Brewery but it was very short lived. Situated by the bridge in Bridge Street it was close to the site of the White Hart Inn and the river, hence its name. Smith was a very clever man who was an orphan brought up by his grandfather but was befriended by Edward Early who paid for his education at Witney Grammar School and the Blue Coat School.

After his education he started work for Early at his mill in Mill Street and rose to the rank of chief inspector. He soon tired of brewing and converted his site into a wool mop making factory for the navy. He realised that there was more money to be made in making blankets and once more converted and expanded his factory to become a great rival to his sponsor's mill. He was very successful in this venture although he was a ruthless

businessman. He was the first to install steam power in the town and this led to a few problems with his workers afraid they would be put out of work. They went on strike and William laid them all off and employed fresh staff. William is now remembered as a blanket maker and very few associate him with brewing, or that Smith's Mill was once a brewery. The site has now been redeveloped for housing and offices.

THE BRITANNIA BREWERY

In 1860, William Gillet founded the Britannia Brewery to the rear of the present Corn Exchange, on the site of which was later to become a Drill Hall and is now Langdale Hall. He sold this at auction at the Fleece Hotel on Tuesday 11 May 1875, along with various tied pubs, stables and a house in West End (possibly the Harriers pub) to the Trustees of William Shuffrey. They in turn later sold out to Hunt Edmunds of Banbury. This brewery took on some of the pubs in their portfolio including the Eagle Vaults, where they may have had a small brewhouse, the Eagle Tavern and the Harriers.

HUDSON'S BREWERY

This small brewery operated during the late 19th century in what is now the West End Industrial Estate. Very little of its history is known for it was probably only a brewhouse for the Union and Nelson pubs. Parts of its foundations and the floor can be seen by the banks of the River Windrush.

OUTSIDE BREWERIES

Apart from the local breweries Witney pubs were also served by, and usually owned by outside Witney breweries. Courage took over all the pubs owned by Clinch's Brewery, but even they have sold out to various companies now. Morrells of Oxford also owned several pubs in Witney before they ceased business. These included the Red Lion and the Rowing Machine who leased it from Whitbread. Morland of Abingdon also had several pubs in Witney until they sold out to Greene King. One of their pubs was the Three Horseshoes which still displays their sign. Garne of Burford also owned the Griffin until they were taken over by Wadworths. Many of Witney's pubs are now owned by major brewers through their own property companies who install managers instead of tenants.

CHAPTER FIVE

Witney Pub Quiz

This chapter may be reproduced for a pub quiz without the permission of the author and publisher. All the answers can be found in this book. It is up to the quiz organiser or reader to find them.

1: What nickname did the locals give the Lamb and Flag?

Answer: ....

2: What was the Bull in Market Square famous for?

Answer: ....

3: Who gave a tapestry to the White Hart?

Answer: ....

4: Where did Fergus O'Conner buy land at Minster Lovell to form his workers' farms?

Answer: ....

5: Which pub was closed in Corn Street in 1906 by the Licensing Committee?

Answer: ....

6: What was the original name of Izi's Bar?

Answer: ....

7: What was the original name of the Marlborough Hotel?

Answer: ....

8: What was the original name of the Plough?

Answer: ....

9: Which inn served no alcohol?

Answer: ....

10: Where did the Clinch Brewery start?

Answer: ....

11: Which brewery now owns the Eagle Tavern?

Answer: ....

12: Windrush Club is situated above which former inn?

Answer: ....

13: Which English King stayed in Witney in 1644?

Answer: ....

14: Where did some Belgian refugees stay in Witney during World War I?

Answer: ....

15: What prestigious award did the Eagle Vaults win in November 2005?

Answer: ....

16: Who brought the Brakspear brewing equipment to Witney?

Answer: ....

17: In which Witney pub did Brakspear Brewery start?

Answer: ....

18: From which pub did the Burford Post Chase start?

Answer: ....

19: Where is Wadworth's only pub in Witney?

Answer: ....

20: A house in West End still has a brewery plaque on its wall. What was this pub's name?

Answer: ....

21: What was the name of the pub that is now the Oxfam shop?

Answer: ....

22: What was the name of the House of Windsor before 1917?

Answer: ....

23: Who was the famous poet who often visited the Fleece?

Answer: ....

24: What is the oldest pub sign in England?

Answer: ....

25: What is the most common name for a pub in England?

Answer: ....

26: Who brought pub signs to England?

Answer: ....

27: Which pub is said to be haunted by a former prisoner?

Answer: ....

28: What was the original name of Norton's?

Answer: ....

29: At the turn of the 20th century how many pubs were there in Witney?

Answer: ....

30: Which famous pop group had lunch in the Windrush Inn?

Answer: ....

Witney Pub Quiz Answers
(But no cheating!)

1   Long Bar
2   Its Darts team
3   Queen Elizabeth I
4   Crown Inn
5   Malt Shovel
6   Hush Bar
7   Blue Boar
8   Plough and Shuttle
9   Temperance Hotel
10 Fleece Hotel
11 Hook Norton
12 King's Arms
13 Charles I
14 Black Horse
15 Best pub in Oxfordshire
16 Wychwood Brewery
17 Cross Keys
18 Holly Bush
19 The Griffin
20 Harriers
21 Sundial
22 King of Prussia
23 Dylan Thomas
24 Chequers
25 Red Lion
26 The Romans
27 Cross Keys
28 Raffles
29 35
30 The Beatles